ENHANCING YOUR REFLECTION

The Ultimate Reflective Tool for Overcoming All Obstacles

Eboni K. Wilson, PhD

Co-written by Diona C. Wilson

AUTHORHOUSE

AuthorHouse™
1663 Liberty Drive
Bloomington, IN 47403
www.authorhouse.com
Phone: 1-800-839-8640

The purpose of this publication is to enhance, educate and allow for personal reflection for the reader. The authors and Beautiful Vision, LLC Publications shall have neither liability nor responsibility to any person or entity with respect to any loss or damage caused or alleged to be caused directly or indirectly by the information, activities or developments contained in this book. If you do not wish to be bound by the above, you may return this book to the Publisher for a full refund.

First published by AuthorHouse   2/24/2011

ISBN: 978-1-4567-4585-1 (sc)
ISBN: 978-1-4567-4584-4 (e)

Library of Congress Control Number: 2011903027

Printed in the United States of America
This book is printed on acid-free paper.

Certain stock imagery © Thinkstock.

Because of the dynamic nature of the Internet, any web addresses or links contained in this book may have changed since publication and may no longer be valid. The views expressed in this work are solely those of the author and do not necessarily reflect the views of the publisher, and the publisher hereby disclaims any responsibility for them.

This book is available at
www.beautifulvision.org

Greetings,

Because we understand your struggles, thoughts and dreams, we created *Enhancing Your Reflection*, for you to build your own personal skills and develop stronger and better goals for the future you see yourself having.

The contents of this workbook will push you in places, but it is all meant for you to really understand your full potential. Think about this…

Have you ever said, "I will never…"

Have you ever been told, "You can't…"

Do you look around you and accept that where you are is where you will stay?

What does your future hold?

Do your actions mirror your future?

What do you have to do to change this?

This is what this workbook is about… YOU!! Get ready to take a journey that only you control and only you can determine how it ends.

Doc

*Please note to get the ultimate experience out of this workbook you should use it in conjunction with *Reflections of a Self Fulfilling Prophecy* by Dr. Eboni K. Wilson.

REFERENCE FOR PARENT AND TEACHERS

This book is aligned to help you address areas which are directly tied to Common Core Standards for English Language Arts and Writing for grades 6-12. We have developed a coding system to allow you to know exactly which standards the questions align to. Below is a key to the coding system:

English Language Arts

Key Ideas and Details – **KID**

1) Read closely to determine what the text says explicitly and to make logical inferences from it; cite specific textual evidence when writing or speaking to support conclusions drawn from the text.
2) Determine central ideas or themes of a text and analyze their development; summarize the key supporting details and ideas.
3) Analyze how and why individual, events, and ideas develop and interact over the course of the text

Craft and Structure – **CAS**

4) Interpret words and phrases as they are used in text, including determining technical, connotative, and figurative meaning, and analyze how specific words choices shapes meaning or tone.
5) Analyze the structure of texts, including how specific sentences, paragraphs, and larger portions of the text relate to each other and the whole
6) Assess how point of view or purposes shapes the content and style of a text

Integration of Knowledge and Ideas – **IKI**

7) Integrate and evaluate content presented in diverse formats and media, including visually and quantitatively as well as in words
8) Delineate and evaluate the argument and specific claims in a text, including the validity of the reasoning as well as the relevance and sufficiency of the evidence.
9) Analyze how two or more texts address similar themes or topics in order to build knowledge or to compare the approaches the authors take.

Range of Reading and Level of Text Complexity – **RTC**

10) Read and comprehend complex literacy and informational texts independently and proficiently.

Writing

Text Types and Purposes – **TTP**

1) Write arguments to support claims in an analysis of substantive topics or texts using valid reasoning and relevant and sufficient evidence
2) Write informative/explanatory texts to examine and convey complex ideas and information clearly and accurately through the effective selection, organization, and analysis of content
3) Write narratives to develop real or imagined experiences or events using effective technique, well-chosen details, and well-structured events sequences.

Production and Distribution of Writing – **PDW**

4) Produce clear and coherent writing in which the development, organization, and style are appropriate to task, purpose, and audience.
5) Develop and strengthen writing as needed by planning, revising, editing, rewriting, or trying a new approach.
6) Use technology, including the Internet, to produce and publish writing and to interact and collaborate with others.

Research to Build and Present Knowledge – **BPK**

7) Conduct short as well as more sustained research projects based on focused questions, demonstrating understanding of the subject under investigation.
8) Gathering relevant information from multiple print and digital sources, assess the credibility and accuracy of each source, and integrate the information while avoiding plagiarism.
9) Draw evidence from literary or informational texts to support analysis, reflection, and research

Range of Writing – **ROW**

10) Write routinely over extended time frames (time for research, reflection, and revision) and shorter time frames (a single sitting or a day or two) for a range of tasks, purposes, and audiences

These standards were obtained from the Common Core State Standards Initiative 2010. To review all the Common Core Standards and which states have already adopted visit http://www.corestandards.org/.

Understanding that Social Emotional growth and development is critical to children's short and long term success, this text is also aligned to CASEL's (Collaborative for Academic, Social, and Emotional Learning) skills and competencies:

1) Self Awareness (**SA**) – Understanding and evaluating your own feelings, likes, values and strengths; and supporting a solid sense of self-confidence
2) Self Management (**SM**) – maintaining your own emotions, handling stress, controlling negative thoughts, overcoming obstacles, setting personal/academic goals and benchmarks for obtaining those goals.
3) Social Awareness (**SoA**) – recognizing and having compassion from others, identifying and understanding similarities and differences with others, identifying and utilizing community resources.
4) Relationship Skills (**RS**) – developing and preserving positive relationships, avoiding peer pressure and poor decisions; steering clear of, handling, and solving interpersonal conflicts; getting help when needed
5) Responsible Decision Making (**RDM**) – using ethics and morals to make decisions, understanding and following social norms, respecting self and others, knowing consequences for your actions, using appropriate decision-making skills in all areas of life, and giving back to school, community and family.

These skills and competencies were obtained from the CASEL website 2010. For more information on these competencies you can visit the CASEL website at http://casel.org/.

INTRODUCTION

1) In reading the title and back cover of the book what do you think *Reflections of a Self Fulfilling Prophecy* is about? (KID1)

_____

_____

_____

_____

_____

_____

_____

2) What does the picture on the front of the book make you think? What do you feel when you see the picture? (SA)

_____

_____

_____

_____

_____

_____

_____

3) Understanding what the back of the book said, what do you think you will learn from this text? (CAS5)

_____

_____

_____

_____

_____

_____

_____

4) In looking at the picture who do you think is shown in the picture? What do you think about him? Describe him? How do you think you are similar to him and different from him? (IKI7)

_____

_____

_____

_____

_____

_____

_____

_____

_____

_____

_____

_____

_____

_____

_____

SECTION I: CHAPTERS I – 5

Chapter I

Vocabulary - Define the following words as they are used in the context of the text (CAS4):

Endeavors: _____

Yearn: _____

Persevering: _____

Prematurely: _____

Collaborated: _____

Executing: _____

Deviant: _____

Socialite: _____

Dominated: _____

1) What is a ghetto? What is life in the ghetto to you? (IKI9)

_____

_____

_____

_____

_____

_____

_____

_____

_____

2) In the boxes below draw three pictures of what the ghetto is to you. (CAS4, TTP3)

3) What does Eboni mean when he says "poverty is a mentality"? What is poverty to you? (CAS5)

_____

_____

_____

_____

_____

_____

_____

_____

_____

4) Eboni said Peanut was conditioned to adapt to his environment for survival what does this mean? Can you relate to this? Why or why not? (IKI8, TTP2)

_____

_____

_____

_____

_____

_____

_____

_____

_____

_____

_____

5) Do you think Eboni is happy? Why or why not? (CAS6)

_____

_____

_____

_____

_____

_____

_____

_____

_____

_____

6) Which one of Eboni's family members can you relate to? Why?(CAS6,SA)

_____

_____

_____

_____

_____

_____

_____

_____

_____

7) Using the Venn diagram, compare and contrast yourself to Eboni and one of his family members below. Be sure to give specific examples. Use one circle for you, one for Eboni and one for one of the other family members. The largest part is how you differ; the intersection is how you are the same. Be sure to give specific information about how you are similar and how you are different. (IKI9, SoA)

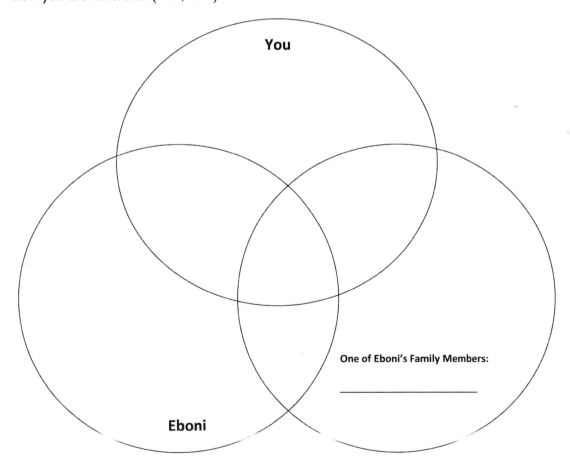

8) Why do you think Eboni said that learning how to reach dreams tangles everything up? (CAS4)

_____
_____
_____
_____
_____
_____
_____
_____
_____
_____
_____
_____
_____
_____

Chapter 2

Vocabulary - Define the following words as they are used in the context of the text (CAS4):

Dynamics: _____

Unselfishness: _____

Squirm: _____

Bewilderment: _____

Petrified: _____

Transpire: _____

Rant: _____

Egged: _____

Patronize: _____

Sabotage: _____

Infuriate: _____

Partaking: _____

Humiliate: _____

Excruciating: _____

Merriment: _____

9) Why did Grandma shoot at Junior and his wife? What other ways do you think she could have handled the situation? How did Eboni feel when this happened? How would you have felt? What would you have done? (KID1, KID3, SA, SoA)

_____
_____
_____
_____
_____
_____
_____
_____
_____
_____
_____
_____
_____
_____
_____
_____

10) What do you think is going to happen between Eboni and Junior? Why do you think this? (KID3,IKI8)

_____
_____
_____
_____
_____
_____
_____
_____
_____
_____
_____
_____
_____
_____
_____
_____

11) How would you have dealt with Junior? How do you deal with family members who you do not like? (KID1,SM,RS)

_____

_____

_____

_____

_____

_____

_____

_____

_____

_____

_____

_____

_____

_____

12) What are four character traits of Grandma? Using the diagram below to show your answers. In the smaller box write the character trait and in the larger box give reasons why or examples of this trait: (KID3, IKI9)

Trait	Examples:

Trait	Examples:

Trait	Examples:

Trait	Examples:

13) What are three character traits of Junior, use the diagram below giving the trait and three examples for each trait (KID1, KID2, IKI7)

Trait: _____

Trait: _____

Trait: _____

14) How did the poem "Your Discipline" make you feel? Why do you feel this way? (SA, SM, SoA)

_____

_____

_____

_____

_____

_____

_____

_____

_____

_____

_____

_____

_____

_____

_____

_____

_____

_____

_____

Chapter 3

Vocabulary - Define the following words as they are used in the context of the text (CAS4):

Miserable: _____

Sanity: _____

Pursuing: _____

Unfathomable: _____

15) What would you do if you were in a home that was unstable and never provided you with the basic necessities of life? (KID2, KID3, SM, RS)

_____

_____

_____

_____

_____

_____

_____

_____

_____

_____

16) What was the cause of Eboni's distancing himself from his family and what was the effect of this action? (KID1, IKI9, RDM)

_____

_____

_____

_____

_____

_____

_____

_____

_____

_____

_____

17) How did Eboni feel when Bernard told others about his "career"? (KID2, SoA)

_____

_____

_____

_____

_____

_____

_____

_____

_____

18) What do you think is going to happen to Eboni? Why do you think this? (CAS4, CAS5)

_____

_____

_____

_____

_____

_____

_____

_____

_____

_____

19) What were Eboni's rules about his "career"? Have you ever had to have a "career" like Eboni? What was it? (KID1, CAS4)

_____

_____

_____

_____

_____

_____

_____

_____

_____

20) Why did Eboni feel good about his life at the end of the chapter? (KID1, KID3, CAS6, IKI8)

_____

_____

_____

_____

_____

_____

_____

_____

_____

_____

_____

_____

_____

_____

_____

_____

_____

_____

_____

Chapter 4

Vocabulary - Define the following words as they are used in the context of the text (CAS4):

Cautious: _____

Infuriated: _____

Hysterical: _____

Bawl: _____

Lurking: _____

Unadulterated: _____

Engulfed: _____

Inferno: _____

Surreal: _____

21) Why do you think Eboni did not care about his grades? What makes you think this? What does school mean to you? Do you care about your school performance? Why or why not? (KID1, CAS6, IKI8, BPK9, SA)

_____

_____

_____

_____

_____

_____

_____

_____

_____

_____

_____

_____

_____

_____

_____

_____

_____

_____

_____

_____

_____

_____

_____

_____

_____

_____

_____

_____

_____

_____

_____

22) Below is a goal setting chart for school. Complete the chart for yourself. Decide what the ultimate goal is and then determine three smaller goals to achieve the ultimate goal and then answer the questions in the boxes for the smaller goals. (TTP3, SA, SM, SoA, RDM)

The Ultimate School Goal: _____

Short Term Goal 1:	Short Term Goal 2:	Short Term Goal 3:
How can I achieve this goal? What do I have to do?	How can I achieve this goal? What do I have to do?	How can I achieve this goal? What do I have to do?
What is stopping my progress in achieving this goal?	What is stopping my progress in achieving this goal?	What is stopping my progress in achieving this goal?
What can I do to overcome this obstacle?	What can I do to overcome this obstacle?	What can I do to overcome this obstacle?

23) What would you have done if your money was taken by your mom or another family member? What do you think about Mama's attitude and reaction to Eboni's questioning? (CAS4, IKI8)

_____

_____

_____

_____

_____

_____

_____

_____

_____

_____

24) What happened to Mama with her boyfriend? (KID1, RTC10)

_____

_____

_____

_____

_____

_____

_____

_____

25) Why does Eboni go to school early? What does he do? Why? What does he learn to do? (KID1, KID3)

_____

_____

_____

_____

_____

_____

_____

_____

26) What did you think was going to happen with the fire? Where do you think the family will live? (KID1)

_____

_____

_____

_____

_____

_____

_____

_____

_____

_____

_____

Chapter 5

Vocabulary - Define the following words as they are used in the context of the text (CAS4)

Salvage: _____

Looming: _____

Grueling: _____

Might: _____

Taunted: _____

Daggers: _____

Burly: _____

Wavering: _____

Generosity: _____

27) Eboni talks about a perfect family, what do you understand that to be? Why? (KID3, IKI8, SA)

_____

_____

_____

_____

_____

_____

_____

_____

_____

28) Create and develop a story about a perfect family. Outline the story below. Be sure to make one of the family members you. Describe each family member and tell how they are so perfect. After you have outlined the story, write the story outside the workbook as a final copy. (TTP3, PDW4, PDW5, ROW, SA)

Beginning
Setting: Time: Place:

Characters:

Problem:

Plot/Events:

Resolution:

29) Give three of Marcos character traits and describe them in the boxes below? What made you choose these traits? (KID1, KID2, IKI7)

Trait:

Trait:

Trait:

30) How do you confront your fears? (SA, SM, RS, RDM)

_____

_____

_____

_____

_____

_____

_____

_____

_____

_____

_____

_____

_____

_____

_____

_____

_____

_____

_____

31) Have you been bullied? What did you do? Have you seen some one get bullied? If so, what did you do? What is your perception of a bully? (SA, SM, SoA, RDM)

_____

_____

_____

_____

_____

_____

_____

_____

_____

_____

_____

_____

_____

_____

_____

_____

_____

_____

_____

_____

_____

_____

_____

_____

_____

_____

_____

_____

_____

_____

_____

_____

_____

32) Eboni seemingly has a carefree-not-afraid-of-anything attitude, do you really think he is like this or that is just how his exterior is? Give three supporting traits that make you feel this way? (KID1, CAS4, IKI8)

_____
_____
_____
_____
_____
_____
_____
_____
_____
_____
_____
_____
_____
_____
_____
_____
_____
_____
_____
_____
_____
_____
_____
_____
_____
_____
_____
_____
_____
_____
_____
_____
_____

Research the following individuals, topics or ideas (TTP2, PDW4, PDW5, BPK7, BPK8, BPK9, ROW10):

- Maya Angelou's poems, life and writings. Analyze one of her poems and write a summary of your analysis then write a poem similar to a Maya Angelou poem (Chapter 1)

- Gun violence (Chapter 2)

- Youth drinking statistics (Chapter 2)

- Bullying, bullying statistics and what kids can do to stop bullying (Chapter 5)

- Research the history of street gangs in America. Compare and contrast the Crips and Bloods, or two other street gangs in your community. Address their positive and negative effects on the community. (Chapter 1) Use the diagram below to help you organize your points.

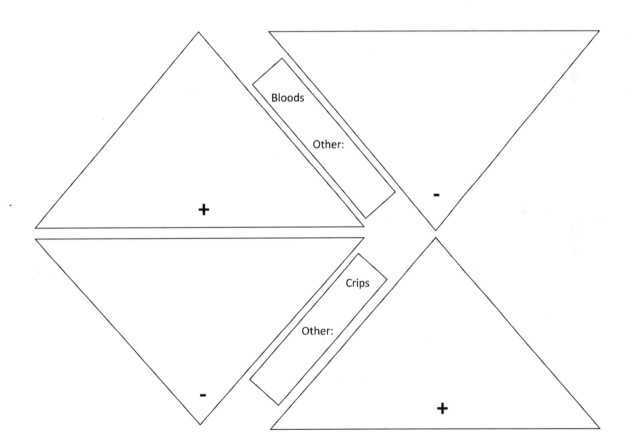

SECTION 2: CHAPTERS 6 – 10

Chapter 6

Vocabulary - Define the following words as they are used in the context of the text (CAS4)

Despised: _____

Splurge: _____

Launch: _____

1) How would you have felt if you found your mom smoking crack? (SA)

_____

_____

_____

_____

_____

_____

_____

_____

_____

_____

_____

2) Do you think Mama cared about Eboni? (KID1, KID3)

_____

_____

_____

_____

_____

_____

_____

_____

_____

_____

_____

3) What would you have done with the large tip the man gave Eboni? (KID2, SA)

_____

_____

_____

_____

_____

_____

_____

_____

_____

_____

4) What is your release? Where can you lose yourself? (SA, SM, RDM)

_____

_____

_____

_____

_____

_____

_____

_____

_____

_____

_____

5) Where is your wonderland? How do you feel when you are there? (SA, SM, RDM)

_____

_____

_____

_____

_____

_____

_____

_____

_____

_____

_____

6) Write a poem about something that you feel is destroying your community. (CAS4, TTP3, ROW10)

_____

_____

_____

_____

_____

_____

_____

_____

_____

_____

_____

_____

_____

_____

_____

_____

_____

_____

_____

_____

_____

_____

_____

_____

_____

_____

_____

_____

_____

_____

_____

_____

Chapter 7

Vocabulary - Define the following words as they are used in the context of the text (CAS4):

Boisterous: _____

Obliged: _____

Convulsions: _____

Delirious: _____

Hypes: _____

Obnoxious: _____

Petrified: _____

Frantic: _____

Emerged: _____

Dispersed: _____

7) How do you deal with your anger? When people make you angry what do you do? What are three positive things you could do when situation is making you angry or frustrated? Complete the activity below. (SA, SM, RS, RDM)

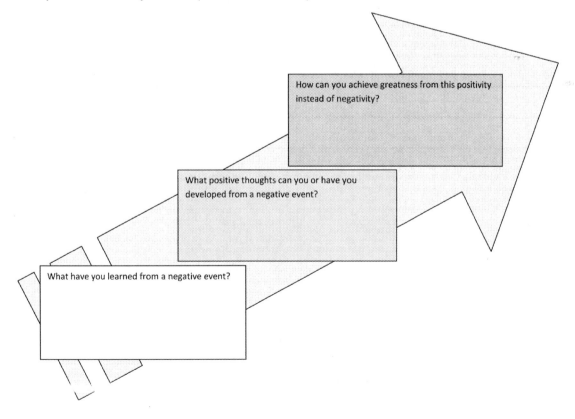

How can you achieve greatness from this positivity instead of negativity?

What positive thoughts can you or have you developed from a negative event?

What have you learned from a negative event?

8) How would you react if a police SWAT team raided you home? What would you do? (KIDI, SA)

_____

_____

_____

_____

_____

_____

_____

_____

_____

9) Discuss how police are viewed in your community. How do you feel about the police? Why? (KIDI)

_____

_____

_____

_____

_____

_____

_____

_____

10) What is your inner peace? How did you discover this? (SA)

_____

_____

_____

_____

_____

_____

_____

_____

Chapter 8

Vocabulary - Define the following words as they are used in the context of the text (CAS4):

Proverbial: _____

Throbbing: _____

11) How does your life (either positive or negative) reflect what is going on around you? (SM, SoA)

_____
_____
_____
_____
_____
_____
_____
_____

12) Do you get into physical fights? Why? Is there a better way to release? If so, what is it? If not, why? (SA, SM, RS, RDM)

_____
_____
_____
_____
_____
_____
_____
_____
_____
_____

13) Do you have someone in your life that plays a similar role like Marcos does to Eboni? Who is it? How do they help you? How do you help him or her? (KID1, KID3, RS)

_____
_____
_____
_____
_____
_____
_____
_____
_____
_____

14) Why do you think Eboni was not happy to see his mom? How would you feel? (KID1, SA)

_____

_____

_____

_____

_____

_____

_____

_____

_____

_____

_____

_____

_____

Chapter 9

Vocabulary - Define the following words as they are used in the context of the text (CAS4):

Extremist: _____

Switch: _____

Ingenious: _____

Ridiculed: _____

15) Who is the boss of you? (SA, SM, RS)

_____

_____

_____

_____

_____

_____

_____

_____

_____

_____

_____

_____

16) How do you celebrate holidays? What rituals do you have in your home or family? (SA, RS)

_____

_____

_____

_____

_____

_____

_____

_____

_____

17) What was your favorite gift? Who bought it? Why was it your favorite? (SA)

_____

_____

_____

_____

_____

_____

_____

_____

_____

18) On page 48, the word Santa was in quotes, why was it in quotes? (KID1, CAS4, CAS5)

_____

_____

_____

_____

_____

_____

_____

_____

_____

19) What does the poem "Ghetto Cry" mean to you? Why? (KID1, KID2, CAS5, RTC, SA)

_____
_____
_____
_____
_____
_____
_____
_____
_____
_____
_____
_____
_____
_____
_____
_____
_____
_____
_____

Chapter 10

Vocabulary - Define the following words as they are used in the context of the text (CAS4):

Gratification: _____

Hesitation: _____

20) Why did Eboni claw his face? Understanding his relationship with his mother, what would you tell Eboni to do? (KID1, KID3, SoA)

_____
_____
_____
_____
_____
_____
_____
_____
_____

21) What is special education? Why was Eboni there? Was it a good place for him to be? Do you think it will help him or hurt him? Do you think this was the right decision for the Principal to make? (KID1)

_____

_____

_____

_____

_____

_____

_____

_____

_____

_____

_____

_____

22) What did special education mean to Eboni? (KID1, KID2, KID3)

_____

_____

_____

_____

_____

_____

_____

23) Do you have a person in your life that is like Ms. Jackson? Why do you feel this way? (SA, RS)

_____

_____

_____

_____

_____

_____

_____

24) Do you think Eboni was right in telling the counselor? Why or why not? What would you have done? (KIDI, SA)

_____

_____

_____

_____

_____

_____

_____

_____

_____

_____

_____

_____

25) Do you believe Eboni was verbally abused? Why or why not? Have you experienced verbal abuse? If so how have you dealt with it? If not what would you do if someone verbally abused you? (SA, RDM)

_____

_____

_____

_____

_____

_____

_____

_____

_____

_____

_____

_____

_____

_____

_____

_____

_____

26) What does it mean to be unfit? (CAS4)

_____

_____

_____

_____

_____

_____

_____

_____

_____

_____

27) What do you have to do to survive? Does this mean you have to make choices you do not like or act in a way you do not agree with? Why? (SA, SM, RDM)

_____

_____

_____

_____

_____

_____

_____

_____

_____

_____

_____

_____

_____

_____

_____

_____

_____

_____

28) Write a story about survival and overcoming an obstacle. Use the graphic organizer below to help outline your story. (TTP3, PDW4, PDW5)

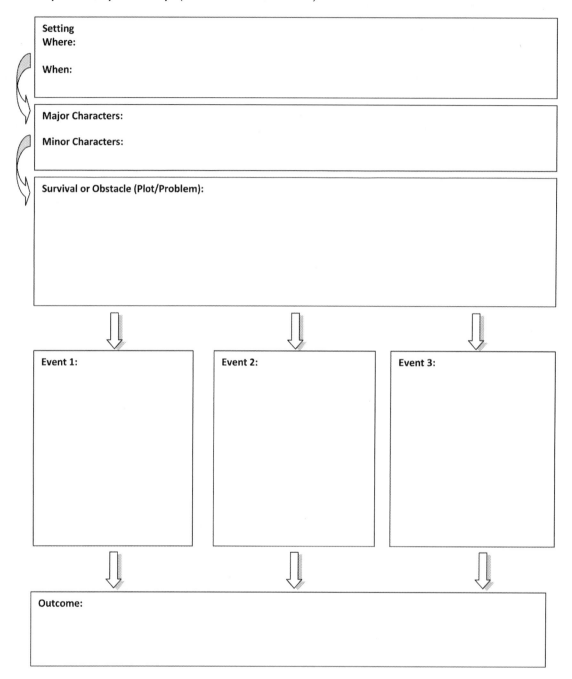

Research the following individuals, topics or ideas (TTP2, PDW4, PDW5, BPK7, BPK8, BPK9, ROW10)

- Research epilepsy and seizures…what are they, what causes them, how do you prevent them (Chapter 7)

- Research overrepresentation in special education, how does this have a relationship to Eboni? Understanding the research on special education overrepresentation what do the statistics say about Eboni's future? (Chapter 10)

SECTION 3: CHAPTERS 11 – 15

Chapter 11

Vocabulary - Define the following words as they are used in the context of the text (CAS4):

Prostituting: _____

Roam: _____

Façade: _____

Raspy: _____

Groped: _____

Molested: _____

1) Why do you think Mama ignored Eboni? (KID1, KID2)

_____

_____

_____

_____

_____

_____

_____

_____

2) How would you feel if you saw your mother prostituting? What would you do? (SA, SM, SoA, RDM)

_____

_____

_____

_____

_____

_____

_____

_____

_____

3) Why was Mama so hostile about giving the children away? (KID1, KID3)

_____

_____

_____

_____

_____

_____

_____

_____

_____

4) Write a poem about living with someone you cannot stand. (TTP3, ROW10)

_____

_____

_____

_____

_____

_____

_____

_____

_____

_____

_____

_____

_____

_____

_____

_____

_____

_____

_____

_____

5) How would you handle the situation with the women behind the church? (SM, RDM)

_____

_____

_____

_____

_____

_____

_____

_____

_____

_____

_____

6) What emotions do you think Eboni felt? How would you have felt? (KID1, KID3, SA)

_____

_____

_____

_____

_____

_____

_____

_____

7) Have you ever been in a situation where you were scared? What did you do? Looking back what would you have done differently? (SM, RDM)

_____

_____

_____

_____

_____

_____

_____

_____

8) Do you think what the woman did behind the church was wrong? Why or why not? (KID1, KID3, RDM)

_____

_____

_____

_____

_____

_____

_____

_____

_____

_____

_____

Chapter 12

Vocabulary - Define the following words as they are used in the context of the text (CAS4):

Garbled: _____

Tirade: _____

Defenseless: _____

Fiasco: _____

9) Why do you think Eboni became withdrawn? (KID1, SoA)

_____

_____

_____

_____

_____

_____

_____

_____

_____

_____

_____

_____

10) Dysfunction is a way to describe Eboni's family. How would you describe your family? Why? Give at least three reasons why you describe your family this way using the diagram below. (KID3, SA, SoA, RS)

Reason 1:

Reason 2:

Reason 3:

11) Eboni recalls the smell of crack, what smells do you associate with your family, home or neighborhood? Is this a good memory or bad? Why? (KID1, KID3, SA, SoA)

_____

_____

_____

_____

_____

_____

_____

_____

_____

_____

_____

_____

_____

_____

_____

_____

12) Did Eboni enjoy interacting with his family when they were on drugs? Why or why not? How would you feel? What would you have done? (KID1, KID3, SA, RDM)

_____

_____

_____

_____

_____

_____

_____

_____

_____

13) The fight between Junior and Mama ended badly, what would you have done in this situation? Recall a situation when you had to act like the adult because the adults were acting like the children. What was the situation? What did you do? How did you feel? Using the six boxes below draw the situation and what happened then use the lines under them to tell the story. (KID3, SA, SM, RDM)

Beginning		

		End

_____

_____

_____

_____

_____

_____

_____

_____

_____

Chapter 13

Vocabulary - Define the following word as it is used in the context of the text (CAS4):

Mimicking: _____

14) Why was Eboni stealing? Do you steal? Is it for necessity or pleasure? Eboni describes it as survival, why? What did he mean? (KID1, KID3, CAS4, CAS5, SA, RDM)

_____

_____

_____

_____

_____

_____

_____

_____

_____

_____

15) What happened when Eboni stole the chain? What is karma? Was this karma? Why or why not? Have you experienced karma? In what situation? How did things end up? What did you learn? (KID1, KID3, SA)

_____

_____

_____

_____

_____

_____

_____

_____

_____

_____

_____

_____

_____

_____

16) Winter was wonderful to Eboni? Why? What did she represent to Eboni? Why did Eboni care about her? (KID1, KID3, CAS5, IKI8, SoA)

_____

_____

_____

_____

_____

_____

_____

_____

_____

_____

_____

_____

_____

_____

_____

_____

17) After Winter died, what did Eboni feel? Why? How would you have felt? What would you have done? (KID1, SA, SoA)

_____

_____

_____

_____

_____

_____

_____

_____

_____

_____

_____

_____

_____

_____

_____

_____

18) Write a poem about losing someone special to you. (TTP3, ROW10, SA, RS)

_____

_____

_____

_____

_____

_____

_____

_____

_____

_____

_____

_____

_____

_____

_____

_____

_____

_____

_____

_____

_____

_____

_____

_____

_____

_____

_____

_____

_____

_____

_____

19) Compare and contrast how you think a family should react when a loved one dies and how Eboni's family reacted to the death of Winter. (CAS4, IKI8, IKI9, TTPI, SoA, RS)

_____

_____

_____

_____

_____

_____

_____

_____

_____

_____

_____

20) What was interesting about Eboni's family grieving together? (KID1, KID3, SoA)

_____

_____

_____

_____

_____

_____

_____

21) Are there certain songs you associate with situations, times or people? What are they? How do they make you feel? (CAS6, SA, SM)

_____

_____

_____

_____

_____

_____

_____

_____

_____

Chapter 14

Vocabulary - Define the following words as they are used in the context of the text (CAS4):

Deteriorate: _____

Belittling: _____

Expire: _____

Fecal Matter: _____

Savior: _____

22) Why do you think Marcos changed? Was he a product of his environment? Why or why not? What does that "product of his environment" mean? (KID1, CAS4)

_____

_____

_____

_____

_____

_____

_____

_____

_____

23) Why do you think Junior and Mama treated Grandma the way they did? What would you have done? How would you have handled the situation? (KID1, KID2, SA, SM)

_____

_____

_____

_____

_____

_____

_____

_____

_____

_____

_____

_____

_____

_____

24) What is arthritis? What does it do to the body? How do you get it? (CAS4)

_____

_____

_____

_____

_____

_____

_____

_____

_____

_____

25) What do you think Mama's dramatics were really about? (KID1, KID3)

_____

_____

_____

_____

_____

_____

_____

_____

_____

_____

26) What were Eboni's dreams signifying? (KID1, KID3, CAS6, IKI8)

_____

_____

_____

_____

_____

_____

_____

_____

_____

27) What does, "I struggled to come to terms with her death and our fate," mean? (CAS4)

_____
_____
_____
_____
_____
_____
_____
_____
_____
_____

Chapter 15

Vocabulary - Define the following word as it is used in the context of the text (CAS4):

Repulsion: _____

28) In your opinion, what is an appropriate timeframe to bury a deceased person? Why do you feel this way? What did Eboni's family do wrong in your opinion? What did they do right? (KID1, SA, SM, SoA)

_____
_____
_____
_____
_____
_____
_____
_____
_____
_____
_____
_____
_____

29) What is cremation? Why do you think Eboni's family had Grandma cremated? (KID1)

_____

_____

_____

_____

_____

_____

_____

_____

30) Why did Eboni have such a hard time with Grandma's death? (KID1, CAS6, SoA)

_____

_____

_____

_____

_____

_____

_____

31) What do you think happens after we die? Why do you feel this way? (SA)

_____

_____

_____

_____

_____

_____

_____

_____

_____

_____

_____

_____

_____

Research the following individuals, topics or ideas (TTP2, PDW4, PDW5, BPK7, BPK8, BPK9, ROW10)

- The history of Goodwill, its mission, purpose and local Goodwill organizations efforts to help your neighborhood (Chapter 11)

- Research drug abuse affects on families (Chapter 12)

- Look into drunk driving statistics in your state with regards to death and children under the age of 18. What are they? What can you do to help change these statistics? Give at least five things (Chapter 13)

SECTION 4: CHAPTERS 16 – 20

Chapter 16

Vocabulary - Define the following words as they are used in the context of the text (CAS4):

Memorializing: _____

Ricocheting: _____

Coherent: _____

Repercussions: _____

Lackadaisical: _____

1) How do you memorialize those you miss? (SA, SM, SoA)

_____

_____

_____

_____

_____

_____

2) Why do you think Eboni thought it was acceptable to rob the man? Was there a difference between him and his brother when it came to this situation? Why do you feel this way? (KIDI, SA, RDM)

_____

_____

_____

_____

_____

_____

_____

_____

_____

_____

_____

_____

3) Have you ever been shot at? How would you feel if you were shot at? What would you do? (KID1, SA, RDM)

_____
_____
_____
_____
_____
_____
_____
_____
_____
_____
_____
_____
_____

4) Where would you go if your family got evicted? (RDM)

_____
_____
_____
_____
_____
_____

5) The first time Eboni sold drugs to a person on the street he was happy? Why was he happy? Do you believe this was a good choice? Why or why not? (KID1, KID2, KID3, RDM)

_____
_____
_____
_____
_____
_____
_____
_____
_____
_____

6) What would you do if you found crack? Why would this be your decision? (SA, RDM)

_____

_____

_____

_____

_____

_____

_____

_____

_____

7) Do you think Eboni will continue to sell crack? Or other drugs? Why or why not? (KID1, CAS4)

_____

_____

_____

_____

_____

_____

_____

_____

_____

_____

8) What do you think Compton will be like for Eboni and his family? Why do you feel this way? (KID1, CAS5)

_____

_____

_____

_____

_____

_____

_____

_____

_____

9) Why do you think Junior's wife has to go to jail for child neglect? Do you think she was neglectful? (KID1, KID3)

_____

_____

_____

_____

_____

_____

_____

_____

10) Eboni talked about Compton being an obstacle? Why does he think this? (KID1, CAS4, CAS6)

_____

_____

_____

_____

_____

_____

_____

_____

11) Eboni wrote a poem about struggling, what do you struggle with? How did this poem make you feel? Why? (KID1, KID3, CAS5, SA)

_____

_____

_____

_____

_____

_____

_____

_____

Chapter 17

Vocabulary - Define the following words as they are used in the context of the text (CAS4):

Theoretically: _____

Enticing: _____

12) Eboni said Jeanie was unstable and had many different personalities? What does this mean? (CAS4)

_____

_____

_____

_____

_____

_____

_____

_____

_____

_____

_____

_____

_____

13) Eboni described the household as one "without a connected purpose," what does he mean? Give three examples. (KID1, CAS4, CAS5)

_____

_____

_____

_____

_____

_____

_____

_____

_____

_____

_____

_____

14) What is walking on eggshells mean? (CAS4)

_____

_____

_____

_____

_____

_____

_____

_____

15) Why did Eboni not want to sell crack? He said it was made to be glamorous, do you feel this way about selling drugs, getting poor grades, being in a gang or something else? Why is it glamorous? (KIDI, CAS4, SA, SoA, RDM)

_____

_____

_____

_____

_____

_____

_____

_____

_____

16) What is enticing to you? (SA)

_____

_____

_____

_____

_____

_____

_____

17) Do you engage in deviant behaviors? Why or why not? (SA, SoA, RDM)

_____

_____

_____

_____

_____

_____

_____

_____

_____

_____

_____

Chapter 18

Vocabulary - Define the following words as they are used in the context of the text (CAS4):

Perplexed: _____

Gratitude: _____

Alluded: _____

Demean: _____

Snuffed: _____

18) Do you believe Eboni's life is really on an upswing? Why do you think this way? (KID1, KID1, KID3)

_____

_____

_____

_____

_____

_____

_____

_____

_____

_____

_____

_____

19) What would you have done if your mother stole from you? (SA, SM, RS, RDM)

_____
_____
_____
_____
_____
_____

20) Bernard's role in Eboni's life started to change; this meant a lot to Eboni, why? What do you think about Eboni's gesture for Bernard's birthday? (KID1, KID2, KID3, SoA)

_____
_____
_____
_____
_____
_____
_____
_____
_____

21) Give three examples of why Eboni called Jeanie Satan and why he said they were "burning in the depths of hell." (KID1, KID3, CAS4, CAS5)

_____
_____
_____
_____
_____
_____
_____
_____
_____
_____
_____
_____

22) Using the Venn diagram below to compare and contrast Eboni's life at 13 or 14 years old to yours. (IKI7, TTP2, SA)

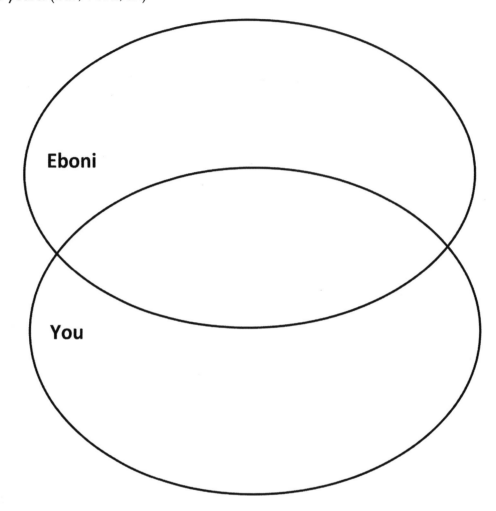

23) Do you believe Eboni's mom is worthless? Why or why not? (KIDI, KID2, KID3)

_____

_____

_____

_____

_____

_____

_____

_____

_____

_____

_____

_____

_____

_____

Chapter 19

Vocabulary - Define the following words as they are used in the context of the text (CAS4):

Unbeknownst: _____

Manhandle: _____

Livid: _____

24) Eboni and Jeanie had a major blow up because of her demanding ways. What would you have done in his situation? Was it worth him losing his home? Why? (KID3, SA, SoA)

_____
_____
_____
_____
_____
_____
_____
_____
_____
_____
_____
_____
_____
_____
_____
_____
_____
_____
_____
_____
_____
_____
_____
_____
_____
_____
_____
_____

25) Why do you think Eboni told Jeanie to kill him? Do you think he was crazy for saying this and feeling that way? Why or why not? Have you ever felt this way? What did you do? (KID1, KID3, SA, SoA, RDM)

_____

_____

_____

_____

_____

_____

_____

_____

_____

_____

_____

26) What emotion do you feel when you think about Eboni's situation? Why? (SA, SoA)

_____

_____

_____

_____

_____

_____

_____

_____

_____

_____

_____

27) Why was Eboni upset about leaving Bernard? (KID1, KID4)

_____

_____

_____

_____

_____

28) Benny was upset with Eboni, why? Do you think he wanted Eboni to live with him? Why? (KID1, KID4)

_____

_____

_____

_____

_____

_____

_____

_____

_____

_____

29) Eboni seemed to like living with Benny, why? If you were Eboni where would you have liked to live? Why? (KID1, SA)

_____

_____

_____

_____

_____

_____

_____

_____

_____

_____

_____

_____

_____

_____

_____

_____

_____

_____

30) Using the table below, identify some of the differences between Eboni's life when he is living with Mama, Jeanie, Benny or by himself. (KID3, TTP2, PDW5, BPK9)

Eboni's Life When Living With...			
Mama	Jeanie	Benny	Himself

Chapter 20

31) Benny called Jeanie to come get Eboni; do you think this was a good decision? Why? (KID1, SoA)

_____

_____

_____

_____

_____

_____

_____

_____

_____

_____

_____

32) Eboni mentioned that his prayers were answered when they found out they were moving. Do you pray? Why or why not? Do you think prayers are really answered or is it just a coincidence? (SA)

_____

_____

_____

_____

_____

_____

_____

_____

_____

_____

33) Eboni said he thought Peanut liked being locked up? Why do you think Eboni felt this way? Do you think this was the truth? Why or why not? Do Peanut's actions hurt Eboni and the rest of the family? Will his actions hurt him in the future? (KID1, KID3, CAS4, SoA)

_____

_____

_____

_____

_____

_____

_____

_____

_____

_____

_____

_____

_____

_____

_____

_____

_____

_____

34) Have you ever been locked up? If so how did you feel? What happened? Did it change how you felt and acted? How or how not? If you have not been locked up, what do you think you would feel? What would you do to avoid that situation in the future? How do you think it would change you? (SA, RDM)

_____

_____

_____

_____

_____

_____

_____

_____

_____

_____

_____

_____

_____

_____

_____

_____

_____

_____

_____

_____

_____

_____

_____

_____

_____

_____

_____

_____

_____

_____

_____

_____

35) Eboni's family got a chance to do right by a couple of recovering addicts, this is like the Pay it Forward theory, write a story about paying it forward and how this idea can change the shape of a community. Use the outline to formulate your thoughts, then use separate paper to write your story form the outline. (CAS4, TTP2, TTP3, PDW4, SoA, RDM)

Setting
Where:

When:

Major Characters:

Minor Characters:

Survival or Obstacle (Plot/Problem):

Event 1:

Event 2:

Event 3:

Outcome:

36) Eboni went to the gym to "escape the madness," while there he said he talked about his suicidal thoughts, why do you think Eboni felt this way? He talks about physical and mental therapy, what did he mean when he said this? What do you do to escape the madness? (KID3, CAS4, SA)

_____

_____

_____

_____

_____

_____

_____

_____

_____

_____

_____

_____

_____

_____

_____

37) Why did Bernard leave? How did this make Eboni feel? Who do you think will be Eboni's support system? (KID1)

_____

_____

_____

_____

_____

_____

_____

_____

_____

_____

_____

_____

_____

_____

38) Have you ever been alone in the context which Eboni describes? If not, what do you do to avoid this feeling? What have you done to escape this feeling? Have you overcome this? (CAS4, SA, SM)

_____

_____

_____

_____

_____

_____

_____

_____

_____

_____

_____

_____

_____

_____

_____

_____

_____

_____

_____

39) Give five positive character traits of Eboni and five negative character traits of Eboni. (KID1, KID3)

Research the following individuals, topics or ideas (TTP2, PDW4, PDW5, BPK7, BPK8, BPK9, ROW10)

- Some cities have gun laws where it is illegal to possess a gun even in your home to protect yourself. Do you agree with this? What are the gun laws in your city or state? If you could create a gun law for you state or city what would it be why? (Chapter 16)

- What is the role of a US Marshall. (Chapter 16)

- What is the difference is between crack and cocaine. What are the possession laws where you live for the different substances (e.g. Marijuana, crack, cocaine)? If Eboni would have got caught in your state with crack what would have happened? (Chapter 16)

- Child Neglect (Chapter 16)

- The Jefferson's was a television series in the late 1970's and early 1980's, this show is regarded as one of the important facets of television history as well as controversial. Why? Give three reasons why it was important in television history and three reasons it was controversial. (Chapter 18)

- Juvenile Halfway homes, what are they, how does a child get placed there. (Chapter 19)

SECTION 5: CHAPTER 21 – 25

Chapter 21

1) Eboni said, "My life began to slide backwards, deeper and deeper into the pit of poverty, anger and dysfunction." Describe what he meant when he said this. (CAS4, CAS5)

_____

_____

_____

_____

_____

_____

_____

_____

_____

_____

_____

_____

_____

_____

_____

_____

_____

_____

_____

_____

_____

_____

2) Eboni was at peace because he was living alone as a 14 year old, imagine you had to live alone, what would you do? Where would you live? How would you eat? Would you continue to go to school? What emotions would you feel? Why do you think Eboni did not go to a shelter? Would you have gone to a shelter? Why or why not? (KID3, SA, SM, RDM)

_____

_____

_____

_____

_____

_____

_____

_____

_____

_____

_____

_____

_____

_____

_____

_____

_____

_____

_____

_____

_____

_____

_____

_____

_____

_____

_____

_____

_____

3) Eboni was alone for two months and said during this time he realized what his mama was really capable of, what does this mean? What are Mama's character traits? Are any of these positive? (KID3, CAS3)

_____

_____

_____

_____

_____

_____

_____

_____

_____

_____

_____

_____

_____

_____

_____

_____

_____

_____

_____

4) What is hustling? Give three examples. Do you have to hustle? Why or why not? (CAS1, SA, RDM)

_____

_____

_____

_____

_____

_____

_____

_____

_____

_____

_____

5) Who is this man in the black Mercedes? Write a story about this man, his life and why you think he tips Eboni so generously (besides him being rich). Use the organizer below to help you organize your thoughts. (KID1, TTP2, TTP3)

Setting
Where:

When:

Major Characters:

Minor Characters:

Survival or Obstacle (Plot/Problem):

Event 1:

Event 2:

Event 3:

Outcome:

6) By the time Eboni spoke to Benny he had been alone for three months. Create a poem about what you think Eboni was thinking during this time or what you would feel in this situation. (KID3, CAS4, TTP3)

_____

_____

_____

_____

_____

_____

_____

_____

_____

_____

_____

_____

_____

_____

_____

_____

_____

_____

_____

_____

_____

_____

7) Why do you think Eboni refused Benny's offer to live with him? (KID1)

_____

_____

_____

_____

_____

_____

_____

8) Describe the situation with Junior's wife, what would you have done? (KID1, KID3, SA, RS)

_____

_____

_____

_____

_____

_____

_____

_____

_____

_____

_____

_____

_____

9) Where do you think Eboni is going? (KID3)

_____

_____

_____

_____

_____

_____

_____

10) Analyze the poem "Survival". (CAS5, CAS6, IKI8)

_____

_____

_____

_____

_____

_____

_____

_____

_____

_____

_____

Chapter 22

Vocabulary - Define the following words as they are used in the context of the text (CAS4):

Reckoned: _____

Tactics: _____

11) What are five character traits of Eboni that determine his approach to life is? Why do you think this? Compare these traits of Eboni to your approach to life? What do you have in common? What are the differences? (KID1, KID3, CAS6, BPK9, SA)

_____

_____

_____

_____

_____

_____

_____

_____

_____

_____

_____

_____

_____

_____

_____

_____

_____

12) Eboni says he was content with his situation, but he was living in a park? Do you think he was really content? Why or Why not? (CAS4, SoA)

_____

_____

_____

_____

_____

_____

_____

_____

13) What is a "screw the world attitude"? (CAS4)

_____

_____

_____

_____

_____

_____

_____

_____

14) Develop a story about living on your own in a park? Where do you sleep? What do you eat? How do you shower and take care of hygiene? Use additional sheets or a story template like previously supplied, if needed. (TTP2, TTP3, PDW4, SA, RDM)

_____

_____

_____

_____

_____

_____

_____

_____

_____

_____

_____

_____

_____

_____

_____

_____

_____

_____

_____

_____

15) Why do you think Eboni ended up calling Benny? What would you have done? (KIDI, SA)

_____

_____

_____

_____

_____

_____

_____

_____

_____

_____

Chapter 23

Vocabulary - Define the following words as they are used in the context of the text (CAS4):

Perpetrating: _____

Adrenaline: _____

16) It seems as though Eboni and Benny have some type of understanding, why do you think this is? What makes Benny different than Mama? (KID3, CAS4, CAS6)

_____

_____

_____

_____

_____

_____

_____

_____

_____

_____

_____

_____

17) Do you think Laron is a good person for Eboni to be with? Why or Why not? (KIDI, RS)

_____

_____

_____

_____

_____

_____

_____

_____

18) Describe the process Eboni talks about when learning to steal a car. (KIDI, CAS4)

_____

_____

_____

_____

_____

_____

_____

_____

19) Eboni was very excited about committing a deviant act, why? Have you experienced this? When? What was the outcome of this excitement? (KIDI, SA, RDM)

_____

_____

_____

_____

_____

_____

_____

_____

_____

_____

_____

_____

20) What is an impulse decision? (MIDI, CAS4, RDM)

_____

_____

_____

_____

_____

_____

_____

_____

Chapter 24

Vocabulary - Define the following words as they are used in the context of the text (CAS4):

Wrath: _____

Impoverished: _____

Balmy: _____

21) Eboni seemed to have the driving of a stolen car down. What was the problem with this process? Give three supporting reasons why this was a problem. (KIDI, CAS4, CAS5)

_____

_____

_____

_____

_____

_____

_____

_____

_____

_____

_____

_____

_____

22) Eboni keeps committing illegal acts. Evaluate at least three illegal acts he has committed, the results and what Eboni learned. (CAS1, KID3, IKI8, TTP1, RDM)

_____

_____

_____

_____

_____

_____

_____

_____

_____

_____

_____

_____

_____

_____

_____

23) Eboni's first run in with the law landed him a week in juvenile detention, why did he describe this as "the worst experience he had ever had"? Give at least three examples. (CAS4, IKI8)

_____

_____

_____

_____

_____

_____

_____

_____

_____

_____

_____

_____

_____

_____

24) Eboni said, "but in the eyes of everyone else, I was just like the rest of them," what does he mean? (CAS4, CAS6)

_____

_____

_____

_____

_____

_____

_____

25) What does "the institution was designed to keep those who had no escape impoverished" mean? What institution is he referring to? What design is he talking about? What are individuals trying to escape? Do you agree with this statement? Why or why not? (CAS4, CAS5, CAS6, SA, SoA)

_____

_____

_____

_____

_____

_____

_____

26) What does "It was a means to entrap people like me in the clutches of life in the ghettos" mean? Who are people like Eboni? What is entrapment in the clutches of the ghettos? Do you agree with this statement? Why or why not? (CAS4, CAS5, IKI8, TTPI, SA, SoA)

_____

_____

_____

_____

_____

_____

_____

_____

_____

27) Eboni's life seems to cycle around and around? What do you believe he has to do to break the cycle? (KID1, KID2, CAS3, IKI8)

_____

_____

_____

_____

_____

_____

_____

_____

_____

_____

28) The poem "Facts" talks about the system. What is the system? (CAS5, TTP1)

_____

_____

_____

_____

_____

_____

_____

_____

_____

_____

_____

Chapter 25

Vocabulary - Define the following words as they are used in the context of the text (CAS4):

Millisecond: _____

Remorse: _____

Beckoned: _____

Intriguing: _____

29) Bernard carried a gun for protection. It seems he is walking the same path as Peanut. Knowing that Eboni looks up to Bernard what affect do you think his actions will have on Eboni's life, decisions and future? (KID3, CAS5, CAS6)

_____

_____

_____

_____

_____

_____

_____

_____

_____

30) Eboni went crazy when the Crips threatened his brother. He said he "saw red" what did he mean? (CAS4)

_____

_____

_____

_____

_____

_____

_____

_____

_____

31) Why was Eboni expelled if what he did was not on school grounds? What is safe passage? (KID1, KID3)

_____

_____

_____

_____

_____

_____

_____

_____

_____

_____

Research the following individuals, topics or ideas (TTP2, PDW4, PDW5, BPK7, BPK8, BPK9, ROW10)

- The McKinney Act. What are the rights of school aged children when it comes to homelessness? (Chapter 21)

- What is a felony? What is the penalty in your state for committing Grand Theft Auto? (Chapter 23)

- What are the statistics of students who get expelled from school? What do you think the relationship is between incarceration and students who get expelled? Why do you think this? (chapter 25)

SECTION 6: CHAPTERS 26 – 30

Chapter 26

Vocabulary - Define the following words as they are used in the context of the text (CAS4):

Affluent: _____

Insecurities: _____

Pummel: _____

1) Why do you think all the black kids hung out together at Eboni's second school? Is this a tendency that you see where you are? Do you do this? Why or why not? (KID3, SA, SM, SoA)

_____

_____

_____

_____

_____

_____

_____

_____

_____

_____

_____

_____

_____

_____

_____

_____

_____

_____

_____

_____

2) Eboni talks about the boy trying to push his buttons, what pushes your buttons? (CAS4, SA, SM, RDM)

_____

_____

_____

_____

_____

_____

_____

_____

3) What is your understanding of why Eboni beat up the boy? (KID3)

_____

_____

_____

_____

_____

_____

_____

4) Do you believe Eboni deserves to get expelled for what he did? Provide at least three supporting details for your belief? (KID3, TTPI)

_____

_____

_____

_____

_____

_____

_____

_____

_____

_____

_____

_____

5) What do you believe the Principal meant when he said, "go back to the ghetto where he belonged"? (CAS4)

_____

_____

_____

_____

_____

_____

_____

_____

_____

_____

_____

_____

_____

_____

6) In the poem "I Want to Grow," Eboni talks about wanting to be what he dreams of. What do you want to grow to be? Do you believe you can do it? What obstacles stand in your way? (CAS5, SA, SM)

_____

_____

_____

_____

_____

_____

_____

_____

_____

_____

_____

_____

_____

_____

Chapter 27

Vocabulary - Define the following words as they are used in the context of the text (CAS4):

Spawn: _____

Paraphernalia: _____

Sanctifying: _____

Impediment: _____

7) What is the story of Eboni's life to this point in the book? Provide three supporting details for your answer. (KID2, CAS5, TTP1, PDW4)

_____

_____

_____

_____

_____

_____

_____

_____

_____

_____

_____

_____

_____

_____

_____

8) Is Eboni a screw up? Why or Why not? (KID3)

_____

_____

_____

_____

_____

_____

_____

_____

9) What is a turning point? Why did Eboni think this was the turning point in his life? (CAS4, CAS5)

_____

_____

_____

_____

_____

_____

_____

_____

_____

_____

10) How was the situation with Sharon similar to Eboni's previous living conditions and how was it different? (KID1, KID3, CAS5)

_____

_____

_____

_____

_____

_____

_____

_____

_____

11) Give three character traits that Sharon, Sharmony and Aretha all possessed. (KID3, PDW4)

_____

_____

_____

_____

_____

_____

_____

_____

_____

12) What would you do if you witnessed what Eboni saw when he came home? (SA, SoA, RDM)

_____

_____

_____

_____

_____

_____

_____

_____

_____

_____

_____

_____

Chapter 28

Vocabulary - Define the following word as it is used in the context of the text (CAS4):

Oblige: _____

13) What is academic rigor? (CAS4)

_____

_____

_____

_____

_____

_____

_____

_____

_____

_____

_____

_____

_____

14) Eboni discussed three things that were consistent in his life, what are three things that are consistent in your life? (CAS4, SA, SM, SoA, RS, RDM)

_____
_____
_____
_____
_____
_____
_____
_____
_____
_____
_____
_____
_____
_____
_____
_____
_____
_____
_____

15) Does Eboni's life look like it is turning around for the positive? Why do you say this? (KIDI, CAS4)

_____
_____
_____
_____
_____
_____
_____
_____
_____
_____
_____
_____
_____
_____
_____

16) How is Renee different than the other women in Eboni's life? Compare and contrast her to Mama, Jeanie and Grandma using the chart below. (KID3, CAS4, IKI8)

Compare Renee' To...	Contrast Renee' To...
Mama	Mama
Jeanie	Jeanie
Grandma	Grandma

17) Analyze the situation that Coach Johnson put Eboni through on the field. What was significant about this situation? What did it mean? (KID3, CAS5)

_____

_____

_____

_____

_____

_____

_____

_____

_____

_____

_____

_____

_____

_____

_____

18) Use the chart to compare and contrast Coach Johnson, Coach Chapel and Benny. (KID3, CAS4, IKI8)

	Coach Johnson	Coach Chapel	Benny
Coach Johnson		Compare / Contrast	Compare / Contrast
Coach Chapel	Compare / Contrast		Compare / Contrast
Benny	Compare / Contrast	Compare / Contrast	

19) Do you think Eboni has what it takes to go to college? Why or Why not? Do you believe you have what it takes to go to college? Why or why not? Give three reasons. (KID1, KID3, SA, RDM)

_____

_____

_____

_____

_____

_____

_____

_____

_____

_____

_____

_____

Chapter 29

Vocabulary - Define the following words as they are used in the context of the text (CAS4):

Escort: _____

Apprehensive: _____

Chaperone: _____

Dumbfounded: _____

Legitimately: _____

20) What is your impression Mr. Jon Douglas? (KID1)

_____

_____

_____

_____

_____

_____

_____

_____

_____

_____

_____

_____

21) Do you think Eboni has what it takes to work at a business like John Douglas'? (KID1, KID2)

_____

_____

_____

_____

_____

_____

_____

_____

_____

_____

_____

_____

_____

22) What do you think is going to happen to Eboni while working at Jon Douglas's business? (KID3)

_____

_____

_____

_____

_____

_____

_____

_____

Chapter 30

Vocabulary - Define the following words as they are used in the context of the text (CAS4):

Leeches: _____

Plagued: _____

Shenanigans: _____

23) Eboni said he felt like he had a destination in life. What is it? What is your destination? Is it positive or negative? How will you get there? What do you need to get there? (KID1, CAS4, SA, SM, RDM)

_____

_____

_____

_____

_____

_____

_____

_____

_____

_____

_____

_____

_____

24) Eboni seems to be trying to break the cycle in his life, but the rest of the family continues to pull him into the same things over and over again. This is a problem… what do you think the solution is to permanently changing this situation? (KID1, KID3, CAS6)

_____

_____

_____

_____

_____

_____

_____

_____

_____

_____

25) Why was Eboni devastated that Renee' left? (KID1)

_____

_____

_____

_____

_____

_____

_____

_____

_____

26) Having Bernard with him always seems to help Eboni, why do you think this is? (KID1, KID3)

_____

_____

_____

_____

_____

_____

_____

_____

27) What does football do for Eboni? (KID1)

_____

_____

_____

_____

_____

_____

_____

_____

28) The situation between Mama and Benny was similar to the situation between Mama and Junior earlier in the book, how? Give three examples? (KID1, KID2, KID3, CAS5, CAS6, TTP1)

_____

_____

_____

_____

_____

_____

_____

_____

_____

_____

29) Give five examples of the shenanigans Eboni was referring to with regards to the family. (TTP1)

_____

_____

_____

_____

_____

_____

_____

_____

_____

_____

30) Do you have sympathy for Eboni and his family? Why or why not? (SA, SoA)

_____

_____

_____

_____

_____

_____

_____

_____

_____

_____

_____

_____

_____

_____

31) Eboni talks about God's bigger plan, what do you think that is for him? Do you believe there is a bigger plan for you? What is it? (KID1, CAS4, CAS6, SA, RDM)

_____

_____

_____

_____

_____

_____

_____

_____

_____

_____

_____

_____

_____

_____

32) Understanding that your thoughts become your words, your words become your actions, your actions become your habits, your habits become your character and your character becomes your destiny. Complete the activity below about your current situation. (SA, SM, RDM)

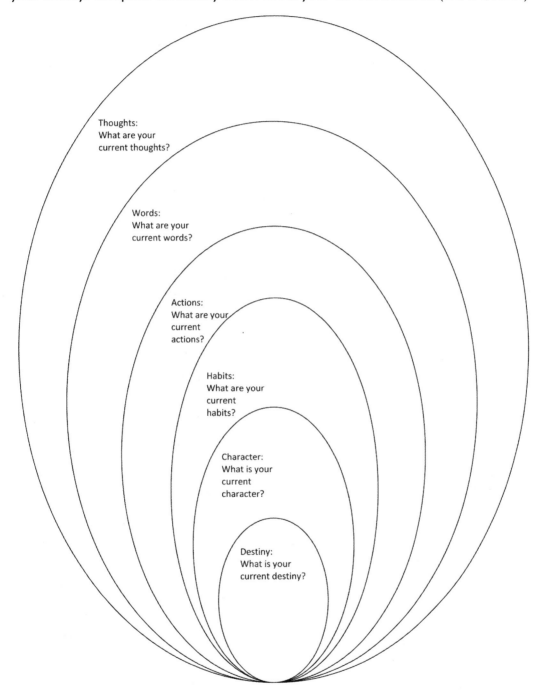

Research the following individuals, topics or ideas (TTP2, PDW4, PDW5, BPK7, BPK8, BPK9, RCW10)

  — The difference in wages for individuals who do not graduate from high school, graduate from high school and graduate from college? Why do you think these differ so much? (Chapter 30)

SECTION 7: CHAPTER 31 – 35

Chapter 31

Vocabulary - Define the following word as it is used in the context of the text (CAS4):

Oxymoron: _____

1) Why do you think Eboni's grades were improving? (KID1)

_____
_____
_____
_____
_____
_____
_____
_____
_____
_____

2) What do you think about Eboni having a girlfriend? Will that help or hurt him? Why do you think this? (KID1, KID3, CAS5)

_____
_____
_____
_____
_____
_____
_____
_____
_____
_____
_____
_____

3) Why do you think Benny married Sharon? (KID1)

_____

_____

_____

_____

_____

_____

Chapter 32

Vocabulary - Define the following word as it is used in the context of the text (CAS4):

Deflated: _____

4) What do you know about the A.C.T.? (KID1, SA)

_____

_____

_____

_____

_____

_____

_____

5) Eboni said he had two people who believed in his future, who were they? Do you think he believed in his future? Why do you say this? (KID1, CAS4)

_____

_____

_____

_____

_____

_____

_____

_____

6) Eboni seemingly has two lives, one positive and one negative. What do you think it will take for him to move totally into the positive areas of his life and leave the negative areas behind? Who contributes to the positive life? Who contributes to the negative life? (KID1, KID3, CAS6, TTP1, SoA)

_____

_____

_____

_____

_____

_____

_____

_____

_____

_____

_____

_____

7) Why do you think Eboni spoke with Jon Douglas about his problem? (KID1)

_____

_____

_____

_____

_____

_____

8) What is ironic about Jon Douglas talking about remembering Eboni? What do you think Eboni means when he says, "God had winked at me"? (KID1, KID2, KID3, CAS4, CAS4)

_____

_____

_____

_____

_____

_____

_____

_____

9) After all the problems Eboni has in LA why do you think he wanted to attend USC? What is so special about USC that made him want to attend? (KID1, CAS4)

_____

_____

_____

_____

_____

_____

_____

_____

_____

_____

_____

_____

_____

_____

10) Do you think Eboni's decision to go to WSU was correct? Why or why not? Where would you have gone? Why? (KID1, SA, RDM)

_____

_____

_____

_____

_____

_____

_____

_____

_____

_____

_____

_____

_____

Chapter 33

Vocabulary - Define the following word as it is used in the context of the text (CAS4):

Plump: _____

11) Did you expect Benny to react the way he did? Why or why not? Did you expect Mama to react the way she did? Why or why not? (KID1, KID2, KID3)

_____
_____
_____
_____
_____
_____
_____
_____
_____
_____
_____
_____
_____
_____
_____
_____

12) What do you believe Coach Johnson, Coach Chapel and Jon Douglas taught Eboni? (KID3, CAS4)

_____
_____
_____
_____
_____
_____
_____
_____
_____

13) What do you think the journey will be for Eboni from this point forward? (KID3, SoA)

_____
_____
_____
_____
_____
_____
_____
_____
_____

14) Write a poem about your destiny. (TTP3, PDW4, SA, SM)

_____
_____
_____
_____
_____
_____
_____
_____
_____
_____
_____
_____
_____
_____
_____
_____
_____
_____
_____
_____
_____
_____

Chapter 34

15) Why do you think Eboni wanted to go to WSU early? (KID1, KID3)

_____

_____

_____

_____

_____

_____

_____

16) Do you think Eboni will see individuals he grew up with again? Why or why not? (KID3)

_____

_____

_____

_____

_____

_____

_____

17) Were you surprised that the family was there to send Eboni off? What do you think about what Bernard told Eboni? Why do you think Bernard looked sad? (KID1, KID2, KID3)

_____

_____

_____

_____

_____

_____

_____

_____

_____

18) What is business management? Do you think this is a good major for Eboni? Why or why not? (KIDI)

_____

_____

_____

_____

_____

_____

_____

_____

_____

19) Do you think there are people in your life who are rooting for your failure? Who? Why? Do you think there are people in your life rooting on your success? Who? Why? What do you think about your future? (SA, SM, SoA, RS)

_____

_____

_____

_____

_____

_____

_____

_____

_____

_____

_____

_____

_____

_____

_____

20) What lessons has Eboni learned early on in college? (KID1)

_____

_____

_____

_____

_____

_____

_____

_____

_____

_____

Chapter 35

Vocabulary - Define the following words as they are used in the context of the text (CAS4):

Vengeance: _____

Retribution: _____

21) Why do you think Eboni referred to Benny as Dad during the phone conversation? (KID2, KID3, CAS4)

_____

_____

_____

_____

_____

_____

_____

_____

_____

_____

_____

_____

_____

_____

22) Eboni had experienced a lot of death in his life, besides his brother, give three reasons why you think this death was particularly hard for him? (KID2, KID3, IKI8)

_____

_____

_____

_____

_____

_____

_____

_____

_____

23) Why do you think he wanted to talk to Benny and not Mama? (KID2, KID3)

_____

_____

_____

_____

_____

_____

_____

_____

_____

_____

24) Do you think Eboni made the right decision to not go home for the funeral? (SoA)

_____

_____

_____

_____

_____

_____

_____

_____

_____

_____

25) While reading this chapter how did you feel? What emotions did it provoke? (SA, SoA, RS)

_____

_____

_____

_____

_____

_____

_____

_____

_____

_____

26) Write a poem about someone special in your life. (TTP2, PDW4, SA, RS)

_____

_____

_____

_____

_____

_____

_____

_____

_____

_____

_____

_____

_____

_____

_____

_____

_____

_____

_____

Research the following individuals, topics or ideas (TTP2, PDW4, PDW5, BPK7, BPK8, BPK9, ROW10)

- Depression and it's affects on relationships (Chapter 31)

- The various options for post secondary education including four year colleges and universities, junior colleges, trade schools, vocational schools, the armed forces, and other educational experiences (Chapter 32)

- The statistics about the number of Black men in college verse the number of black men who are incarcerated (be sure to compare the age group of 17-25) not all individuals. Is it what you expected? Why or why not? Is this what the media portrays? Why do you think this is? (Chapter 34)

SECTION 8: CHAPTER 36 – 40

Chapter 36

Vocabulary - Define the following words as they are used in the context of the text (CAS4):

Frantically: _____

Paralyzed: _____

Rationalize: _____

Internalizer: _____

Avenge: _____

Spiteful: _____

1) Eboni said in his dream the faces were like blank canvases, what does this mean? (CAS4)

_____

_____

_____

_____

_____

_____

2) Eboni said that Benny was an internalizer? What does this mean? What is the difference between externalizing and internalizing? Which are you? (KID2, KID3, CAS4, SA, SM)

_____

_____

_____

_____

_____

_____

_____

_____

_____

_____

_____

3) The whole family seemingly had the same emotions, but reacted differently. Eboni's reaction is not clearly defined, but Eboni had reoccurring dreams about Bernard why do you think this was? He said Bernard was his angel, do you think you have an angel? If so, who is it and why do you think they are your angel? If not why do you think this? (KID2, KID3, CAS5, SA, SOA, RS)

_____

_____

_____

_____

_____

_____

_____

_____

_____

_____

_____

_____

_____

_____

_____

_____

_____

_____

_____

4) What were Bernard's traits? Give at least five traits in the ovals below. (KID3)

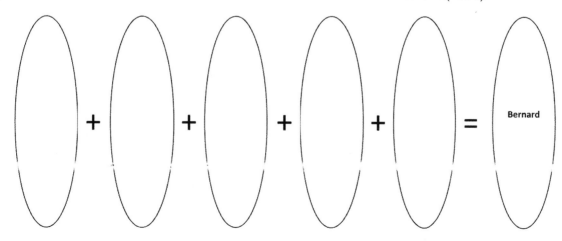

5) The last two chapters were emotional ones for Eboni; recall a situation that was as emotional for you. What was it? How did you react? What did you do? How have you move forward since? (SA, SM, SoA)

_____

_____

_____

_____

_____

_____

_____

_____

_____

_____

_____

_____

_____

_____

Chapter 37

6) What did Eboni mean when he said he felt like every one of his breaths was a little shallower? (CAS4)

_____

_____

_____

_____

_____

_____

_____

_____

_____

_____

7) Why do you think Eboni's studies suffered? He said his tutors were his life lines, what does that mean? (KID1, KID3, CAS4, SoA)

_____

_____

_____

_____

_____

_____

_____

_____

_____

8) Do you think Eboni dating Anna is a good thing for him and what he is trying to do at school? Why or why not? (KID1, TTP1)

_____

_____

_____

_____

_____

_____

_____

_____

9) Why do you think Eboni did not want to go home for the holidays? Give three reasons. (KID1, KID3)

_____

_____

_____

_____

_____

_____

_____

_____

_____

_____

_____

_____

10) Eboni said his joy and security was away from his family and that he had run away from it, apply this thought process to your life, what do you run away from? Why? (CAS4, SA, SM, RDM)

_____

_____

_____

_____

_____

_____

_____

_____

_____

_____

_____

_____

_____

_____

Chapter 38

Vocabulary - Define the following word as it is used in the context of the text (CAS4):

Ecstatic: _____

11) Why do you think Eboni was bringing Travie up to WSU? (KID1, KID3)

_____

_____

_____

_____

_____

_____

_____

_____

_____

_____

12) Do you think Eboni's thoughts about not wanting to get married were realistic? Why? (KID1)

_____
_____
_____
_____
_____
_____
_____
_____
_____
_____
_____

13) Eboni receiving his scholarship was a big deal to him, why? (KID1, KID3)

_____
_____
_____
_____
_____
_____
_____
_____
_____
_____

14) Why did Eboni ignore contact with his family? (KID1, KID3)

_____
_____
_____
_____
_____
_____
_____
_____
_____

Chapter 39

Vocabulary - Define the following words as they are used in the context of the text (CAS4):

Tremendous: _____

Excruciating: _____

Groggy: _____

15) Did you think Eboni and Anna were going to break up? (KIDI, SoA)

_____
_____
_____
_____
_____
_____
_____
_____
_____
_____
_____
_____
_____
_____

16) Did you think Eboni was going to get hurt? (KIDI, SoA)

_____
_____
_____
_____
_____
_____
_____
_____
_____
_____
_____
_____
_____
_____

17) Eboni seems to have a good outlook on the things that have happened to him since going to college, how is this different from when he was a child growing up? Why do you think this? (KID2, CAS5, IKI8)

_____

_____

_____

_____

_____

_____

_____

_____

_____

_____

_____

_____

_____

_____

_____

_____

18) Have Eboni's character traits changed since he left LA? What are they or why do you think he is the same? (KID2, KID3, CAS4, IKI8)

_____

_____

_____

_____

_____

_____

_____

_____

_____

_____

_____

Chapter 40

Vocabulary - Define the following words as they are used in the context of the text (CAS4):

Amputate: _____

Prosthetic: _____

Staph Infection: _____

Stages of Acceptance: _____

Feisty: _____

19) Eboni went through a lot of emotions when the doctors were trying to figure out why he would not stop bleeding, what would you have thought? Would you have felt like Eboni? If so, why? If not why not and what would you have felt? (SA, SM)

_____

_____

_____

_____

_____

_____

_____

_____

_____

_____

_____

_____

20) Do you think Fumi is a good woman for Eboni? Why or Why not? (KID1, KID3, SOA)

_____

_____

_____

_____

_____

_____

_____

_____

_____

_____

21) When attending the Rose Bowl, why do you think Eboni did not let his family know he was there? Why did he call the WSU football team his new family? (KID1, KID3)

_____

_____

_____

_____

_____

_____

_____

_____

_____

_____

Research the following individuals, topics or ideas (TTP2, PDW4, PDW5, BPK7, BPK8, BPK9, ROW10)

- Staph Infections – what are they, how do you get them, how are they cured, where do you get them, can you die from them? (Chapter 40)
- The stages of acceptance, what are they, explain them, have you gone through them, give an example of a situation where someone might go through these stages. (Chapter 40)

SECTION 9: CHAPTERS 41 – 45

Chapter 41

Vocabulary - Define the following words as they are used in the context of the text (CAS4):

Gurney: _____

Paralysis: _____

1) Eboni's spinal cord injury resulted in him not being able to play football again, Eboni said he needed a new outlet, what do you think it will be? Why do you think that he needed this outlet? (KID3, CAS6)

_____

_____

_____

_____

_____

_____

_____

_____

2) Eboni has had many battles from the start of his life, until now, what do you think fuels him to keep going and not give up? What would you do? Can you relate to Eboni and what he has gone through why or why not? What fuels you? (KID3, SA, SoA)

_____

_____

_____

_____

_____

_____

_____

_____

_____

_____

_____

3) It seems that for every step forward Eboni takes he end up going back three steps, what do you think will happen to keep him moving forward instead of backwards? (KID2, CAS6, TTP1)

_____

_____

_____

_____

_____

_____

_____

_____

_____

_____

Chapter 42

Vocabulary - Define the following words as they are used in the context of the text (CAS4):

Yield: _____

Increments: _____

Provisional: _____

Merge: _____

4) Eboni said he came from nothing and had nothing? Do you believe that he had nothing? Why or why not? Where do you come from? (KID1, KID2, KID3, SA)

_____

_____

_____

_____

_____

_____

_____

_____

_____

_____

5) Do you believe it is possible to make that much money so fast legally? (KID1)

_____

_____

_____

_____

_____

_____

_____

_____

6) Eboni said he did not know what a college degree meant, what do you think a college degree means? (KID1, KID2)

_____

_____

_____

_____

_____

_____

_____

_____

_____

7) What does Eboni mean when he said he did not want to study psychology because of the clinical application? (KID1, CAS4, CAS6)

_____

_____

_____

_____

_____

_____

_____

_____

_____

_____

8) Five years earlier Eboni did not think he was college bound, he never had even thought about college, now he is going to graduate school. What do you think drives Eboni to go beyond what he thought he could do? (KID2, KID3, CAS4)

_____

_____

_____

_____

_____

_____

_____

_____

_____

_____

_____

_____

_____

9) Do you think Eboni should have invited his family to his graduation festivities? Why do you feel this way? (KID3, CAS6, TTPI, SoA)

_____

_____

_____

_____

_____

_____

_____

_____

_____

_____

_____

_____

_____

Chapter 43

Vocabulary - Define the following word as it is used in the context of the text (CAS4):

Symbolized: _____

10) Eboni described how he felt when he had the diploma and walked the stage, how do you think you will feel when your day to walk the stage comes? (KID1, KID3, CAS4, SA, SoA)

_____

_____

_____

_____

_____

_____

_____

_____

_____

11) Did you think that Mama was going to take Eboni's items? (KID2, KID3)

_____

_____

_____

_____

_____

_____

_____

12) Eboni noted Mama's "ghetto fabulous 'hood mentality" what do you think he is referring to? (CAS4)

_____

_____

_____

_____

_____

_____

13) Do you think Eboni should blame Travie? Why or why not? (KID1, KID3, CAS6)

_____
_____
_____
_____
_____
_____
_____

14) Do you think Eboni meant it when he said that he never needed to see his Mama again? Why or why not? (KID1, KID3)

_____
_____
_____
_____
_____
_____
_____

15) What does the poem "Perseverance" mean to you? (SA)

_____
_____
_____
_____
_____
_____
_____

Chapter 44

Vocabulary - Define the following word as it is used in the context of the text (CAS4):

Fathomed: _____

16) Would you have spoken to your mom after graduation? Why or why not? (SA, RS)

_____

_____

_____

_____

_____

_____

_____

17) Do you think Eboni should have made decisions based on what Fumi was doing? Why or why not? (KID1, KID3, SoA)

_____

_____

_____

_____

_____

_____

_____

_____

18) What jobs do you think Eboni could get with the type of interests he has and the degrees he has worked for? (KID1, KID3, SoA)

_____

_____

_____

_____

_____

_____

_____

_____

_____

_____

Chapter 45

Vocabulary - Define the following word as it is used in the context of the text (CAS4):

Giddy: _____

19) Coach Price suggested that Eboni work towards a PhD. Why? Do you think Fumi was right when she reassured Eboni? Why or why not? (KID1, KID2, KID3)

_____

_____

_____

_____

_____

_____

_____

_____

_____

_____

_____

_____

_____

_____

_____

_____

_____

_____

_____

_____

_____

_____

_____

_____

_____

20) Eboni said, "for so long I had been broken of my inner confidence and told that I couldn't or I wouldn't or I shouldn't, that I never realized that instead of feeding into negative expectations others had for me, I should have used it as a motivator to prove them wrong," what is he talking about? Give some examples. Later in the chapter this happens again, what is this situation? How does this quote relate to you? (KD1, KID3, CAS4, TTP1)

_____

_____

_____

_____

_____

_____

_____

_____

_____

_____

_____

_____

_____

_____

_____

_____

_____

_____

_____

_____

_____

_____

_____

_____

_____

_____

_____

_____

_____

Research the following individuals, topics or ideas (TTP2, PDW4, PDW5, BPK7, BPK8, BPK9, ROW10)

- The history of the stock market (Chapter 42)
- The PhD process, what is a dissertation? What does it mean for a professional? What would you get your PhD in? Why? (Chapter 45)
- FAFSA and financial aid (Chapter 45)

SECTION 10: CHAPTER 46 – 50

Chapter 46

Vocabulary - Define the following words as they are used in the context of the text (CAS4):

Soliloquy: _____

Ethnographic: _____

Naysayers: _____

1) Eboni noted he was confident in his ability to complete the work, how is this different than his previous educational experiences? (KID1, KID3)

_____

_____

_____

_____

_____

_____

_____

_____

_____

_____

_____

_____

_____

_____

_____

_____

_____

_____

_____

_____

_____

2) Eboni talks about his feelings for Fumi and wanting to marry her, do you think this is a good idea? Why or why not? He discusses how his thought process changed from "me to us" what does that mean? (CASI, KID3, CAS4)

_____

_____

_____

_____

_____

_____

_____

_____

_____

_____

3) What do you think motivated Eboni through this process? (KID3)

_____

_____

_____

_____

_____

_____

_____

_____

_____

Chapter 47

Vocabulary - Define the following words as they are used in the context of the text (CAS4):

Gamut: _____

Graciously: _____

4) Do you think what WSU athletic department did to Eboni was wrong? Why or why not? (KID1)

_____

_____

_____

_____

_____

_____

_____

_____

_____

_____

_____

5) What is a productive member of society? (CAS4)

_____

_____

_____

_____

_____

_____

_____

_____

_____

_____

_____

Chapter 48

Vocabulary - Define the following word as it is used in the context of the text (CAS4):

Skeptical: _____

6) Eboni's process for determining his future with the job in Chicago was one which would take him away from Fumi, is that a good or bad decision? (KID1, KID3)

_____

_____

_____

_____

_____

_____

_____

_____

_____

_____

7) When Eboni told Benny, Mama and Travie about his decision they had nothing but good things to say, is this unusual? What do you think changed? Why did they change? (KID1, KID2, KID3, IKI8)

_____

_____

_____

_____

_____

_____

_____

_____

_____

_____

_____

_____

_____

_____

_____

Chapter 49

Vocabulary - Define the following word as it is used in the context of the text (CAS4):

Ecstatic: _____

8) What challenges do you think Eboni faces now moving across the country by himself? (KIDI, IKI8)

_____

_____

_____

_____

_____

_____

9) Why do you think Eboni and Fumi grew apart? (CASI, CAS3)

_____

_____

_____

_____

_____

_____

10) Eboni said, "learning to be one with someone else you have to be one with yourself," what does that mean? (KIDI, CAS4)

_____

_____

_____

_____

_____

_____

_____

_____

_____

_____

_____

11) Eboni talks about internal focus, what is this? (KID1, CAS4)

_____

_____

_____

_____

_____

_____

_____

12) Eboni's career seems to be taking off, what has previously occurred during positive situations in his life? Do you think this is going to happen again? Why or why not? (KID1, KID3)

_____

_____

_____

_____

_____

_____

_____

_____

_____

_____

_____

_____

_____

_____

13) Who does Eboni have to turn to for help, strength and advice, now that Fumi is no longer in his life? (CAS1, CAS3)

_____

_____

_____

_____

_____

_____

14) What do you think about what Travie said to Eboni? (KID1, KID3, CAS4, SoA)

_____

_____

_____

_____

_____

_____

_____

_____

Research the following individuals, topics or ideas (TTP2, PDW4, PDW5, BPK7, BPK8, BPK9, ROW10)

- Create your resume (Chapter 47)

- Seattle, Washington (Chapter 47)

- Charter schools and the charter school movement. What are the advantages and disadvantages to them? (Chapter 48)

- Chicago, Illinois (Chapter 48)

SECTION 11: CHAPTERS 51 – 55

Chapter 51

Vocabulary - Define the following words as they are used in the context of the text (CAS4):

Heralded: _____

Adversarial: _____

Gawked: _____

1) Eboni talks about Longwood being his comfort zone, what does that mean? What is your comfort zone? (KID1, KID3, CAS4, SA, SM)

_____

_____

_____

_____

_____

_____

_____

_____

_____

_____

_____

_____

2) How did Eboni gain the respect of the students? Why did the staff not like him? (KID1, KID3)

_____

_____

_____

_____

_____

_____

_____

_____

_____

_____

3) The allegations that the young girl made against Eboni pushed him to an emotional breaking point, why? What would you have done? Eboni was depressed and his health was deteriorating, discuss how negativity can affect you not only emotionally, but physically, spiritually, financially and mentally. (KID1, KID2, KID3, SA, SM, SOA)

_____

_____

_____

_____

_____

_____

_____

_____

_____

_____

_____

_____

_____

4) After the girl recanted her story Eboni talks about the excitement he felt, but more about how the lesson was not about him, but the young lady feeling she had to lie to escape being in trouble, do you find this to be a fact? Why or why not? (KID1, KID3, CAS5, SA, SoA, RDM)

_____

_____

_____

_____

_____

_____

_____

_____

_____

_____

_____

_____

5) How did Eboni become stronger from the situation? Give three reasons. (KID3, IK18)

_____

_____

_____

_____

_____

_____

_____

_____

_____

_____

_____

_____

_____

6) In "My Soul Cries" Eboni talks about breaking the standard, what does that mean to you? (CAS4, SA, SM)

_____

_____

_____

_____

_____

_____

_____

_____

_____

_____

_____

_____

_____

Chapter 52

7) Why do you think Eboni wanted a transfer? Does this seem like he was defeated even though the charges were dropped? (KIDI, KID3, TTPI)

_____

_____

_____

_____

_____

_____

_____

_____

_____

8) Eboni's interview as Director of a new school seemed to be just what he wanted; do you think this is a good position for him after what he had gone through in Chester? (KIDI, KID3)

_____

_____

_____

_____

_____

_____

_____

_____

_____

9) Would you have called Mr. Lang to get Travie a job like Eboni did? Why or Why not? (SA, RS, RDM)

_____

_____

_____

_____

_____

_____

_____

_____

Chapter 53

10) Eboni seemed excited about his new position to build lasting relationships with students and work in the city where he started his education career, every time things seem to be good for Eboni, things seemingly go wrong. Do you foresee any problems for Eboni with this position? What are they? Why do you say this? (KID1, KID3, CAS5, IKI8)

_____

_____

_____

_____

_____

_____

_____

_____

_____

_____

11) Eboni bought his first home after starting at Ellison, was this smart? Owning a home is the American dream for some, why do you think it meant so much to Eboni? Give three reasons. (KID1, KID3, IKI8)

_____

_____

_____

_____

_____

_____

_____

_____

_____

_____

Chapter 54

Vocabulary - Define the following word as it is used in the context of the text (CAS4):

Bureaucracy: _____

12) Eboni says he was growing personally, how do you think he has grown? (KID1, KID2, KID3)

_____

_____

_____

_____

_____

_____

_____

_____

_____

_____

_____

_____

13) Eboni made a lot of money in the stock market, what would you have done with this money? (SA, RDM)

_____

_____

_____

_____

_____

_____

_____

_____

_____

_____

_____

_____

14) Eboni talks about making it, what does he mean? How will you know that you have made it? What goals will you have to achieve to make it? (KID3, CAS 4, SA, SM)

_____

_____

_____

_____

_____

_____

_____

_____

_____

_____

_____

_____

_____

_____

_____

_____

_____

_____

_____

_____

_____

Chapter 55

Vocabulary - Define the following words as they are used in the context of the text (CAS4):

Volatile: _____

Unionizing: _____

Optimist: _____

Pessimist: _____

15) Eboni has reached every goal he has set, some which have taught him some lessons, in your opinion, what are three major lessons that Eboni has learned? (KID3, IKI8, SoA)

_____

_____

_____

_____

_____

_____

_____

_____

_____

_____

_____

_____

_____

_____

_____

_____

_____

_____

_____

_____

_____

_____

_____

_____

_____

_____

_____

_____

_____

16) Describe the progression of each of the following characters throughout the course of the book: Travie, Peanut, Mama, Benny. Give characteristics of each individual from the start of the book to the end of the book; remember to address how they progressed. (KID3, IKI8)

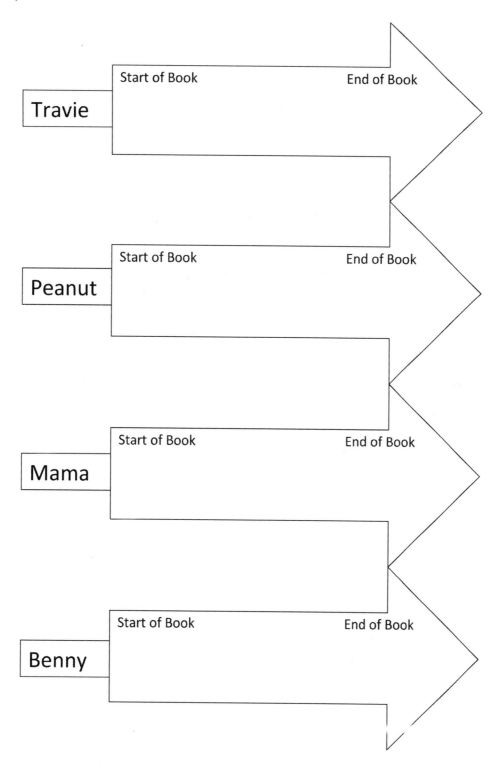

17) Why do you think Eboni still struggles with the relationship he has with Mama? He talks about understanding her mentality, what do you think that mentality is? (KID1, KID3, SA, SoA)

_____

_____

_____

_____

_____

_____

_____

_____

_____

_____

18) Eboni says he has learned to respect the journey Benny has traveled what does this mean? (KID3, CAS4)

_____

_____

_____

_____

_____

_____

19) How does the mind control your perceptions? (KID4, SA, SM, SoA, RDM)

_____

_____

_____

_____

_____

_____

_____

_____

_____

20) Are you an optimist or pessimist? Why? (SA)

_____

_____

_____

_____

_____

_____

_____

_____

_____

_____

21) What does Eboni mean when he says, "the hood is like a waterfall"? (CAS4, IKI8)

_____

_____

_____

_____

_____

_____

_____

_____

_____

_____

22) Who believes in you? Do you believe in you? Why or why not? (SA, SoA, RS)

_____

_____

_____

_____

_____

_____

_____

_____

_____

_____

_____

23) How will you use the obstacles you face to make you stronger? (SA, SM, RDM)

_____
_____
_____
_____
_____
_____
_____
_____
_____
_____
_____
_____

24) What does Eboni mean when he says, "standing still is very different than still standing"? (CAS4)

_____
_____
_____
_____
_____
_____
_____
_____

25) Who are your friends? Who and what are your enemies? What are "frienemeies"? (SA, SM, SoA, RS, RDM)

_____
_____
_____
_____
_____
_____
_____
_____

26) Why is pain temporary and misery optional? What does this mean? (CAS4, CAS5)

_____

_____

_____

_____

_____

_____

_____

_____

27) Who are your haters? Why do they hate? How can you use their hating to motivate you? (SA, SoA)

_____

_____

_____

_____

_____

_____

_____

_____

_____

_____

28) What are wicked desires? What are your blessings? (CAS4, SA, SoA)

_____

_____

_____

_____

_____

_____

_____

Research the following individuals, topics or ideas (TTF2, FDW4, FDW5, BPK7, BPK8, BPK9, ROW10)

- Chester, Pennsylvania (Chapter 51)

REFLECTIONS

1) The start of the book there is a definition of a Self Fulfilling Prophecy. Why do you think the book is entitled *Reflections of a Self Fulfilling Prophecy*? Do you believe in Self Fulfilling Prophecy? Have you framed your life in a 'self fulfilling prophecy' way, either positive or negative? (TTPI, TTP2, PDW4, SA)

_____

_____

_____

_____

_____

_____

_____

_____

_____

_____

_____

_____

_____

_____

_____

_____

_____

_____

_____

_____

_____

_____

_____

2) Think back to how Eboni was at the start of the book. How did he evolve? How did he stay the same? How is he like you? How is he different? How does his story motivate you? How does it disappoint you? (KID2, KID3, IKI8, TTPI, TTP3, SA, SM)

_____
_____
_____
_____
_____
_____
_____
_____
_____
_____
_____
_____
_____
_____
_____
_____
_____
_____
_____
_____

3) Why do you think Eboni wrote this book? What was his approach? (KID3, IKI8, TTP3, PDW4)

_____
_____
_____
_____
_____
_____
_____
_____
_____
_____
_____
_____

4) Create a timeline of your life, starting where you are today, and projecting to twenty years from today. Use the chart below.

Year	Event or Goal to Accomplish
Today	
10 Years from Now	
20 Years from Now	

5) What do you think was the climax of the story? Why do you think this? (KID2)

_____

_____

_____

_____

_____

_____

_____

_____

_____

6) Eboni had motivation to get out of the 'hood and prove every one wrong, what motivates you? Why is this a motivator? What are your 'stepping stones' of motivation? (SA, SM, SoA)

_____

_____

_____

_____

_____

_____

_____

_____

_____

_____

_____

_____

_____

_____

_____

_____

_____

_____

7) What do you believe your assignment to be? (SA, SR, RDM)

_____

_____

_____

_____

_____

_____

_____

_____

_____

_____

8) How are you a seed of greatness and a person of destiny? (SA, SM, RDM)

_____

_____

_____

_____

_____

_____

_____

_____

_____

9) How will you embrace beyond what you see? How will you create a path of your own destiny? (SA, SM, RDM)

_____

_____

_____

_____

_____

_____

_____

_____

_____

_____

_____

_____

_____

_____

_____

_____

_____

_____

10) What is the power of education? (TTP1, PDW4)

Vocabulary and Notes

ADDITIONAL SUPPORTS AND RESOURCES

The following pages are resources for students to use that will help them set goals, reach their goals and maximize their time while working towards a better self and future. There are additional resources on line. Access them through www.beautifulvision.org. Register and then go to the secure area under the EYR tab.

Below is a time management chart to use to organize your daily activities and to help establish a routine for yourself. There is also a goal setting tool to help you establish your goals as well as keep track of your progress towards those goals.

Time Management Table

	Sunday	Monday	Tuesday	Wednesday	Thursday	Friday	Saturday
5:00 – 5:30							
5:30 – 6:00							
6:00 – 6:30							
6:30 – 7:00							
7:00 – 7:30							
7:30 – 8:00							
8:00 – 8:30							
8:30 – 9:00							
9:00 – 9:30							
9:30 – 10:00							
10:00 – 10:30							
10:30 – 1:00							
11:00 – 1:30							
11:30 – Noon							
Noon – 12:30							
12:30 – 1:00							
1:00 – 1:30							
1:30 – 2:00							
2:00 – 2:30							
2:30 – 3:00							
3:00 – 3:30							
3:30 – 4:00							
4:00 – 4:30							
4:30 – 5:00							
5:00 – 5:30							
5:30 – 6:00							
6:00 – 6:30							
6:30 – 7:00							
7:00 – 7:30							
7:30 – 8:00							
8:00 – 8:30							
8:30 – 9:00							
9:00 – 9:30							
9:30 – 10:00							
10:00 – 10:30							
10:30 – 11:00							

Goal Management Tool

Use the goal setting tool below to set a long term goal for yourself. Use the benchmark goal boxes to set short term goals for yourself to meet your long term goal. Refer back to this sheet regularly to ensure you meet your targeted goal.

Goal:

Timeline (When will the goal be accomplished):

Benchmark 1:	Benchmark 2:	Benchmark 3:	Benchmark 4:
Targeted Completion Date: Actual Completion Date:	Targeted Completion Date: Actual Completion Date:	Targeted Completion Date: Actual Completion Date:	Targeted Completion Date: Actual Completion Date:

Draw a picture of how you feel because you have accomplished your goal.

What did you do that helped you achieve your goal?

How did you know you accomplished you goal?

What new goal has developed from you accomplishing this goal?

How will you work to meet this new goal?